Sawhorse

Tony Burfield

Sawhorse
© 2017, Tony Burfield

No part of this book may be reproduced by any means known at this time or derived henceforth without written permission of the publisher or author. The exception would be in the case of brief quotations embodied in the critical articles or reviews and pages where permission is specifically granted by the publisher or author.

Books may be purchased in quantity and/or special sales by contacting the publisher. All inquiries related to such matters should be addressed to:

Middle Creek Publishing & Audio
9027 Cascade Avenue
Beulah, CO 81023
editor@middlecreekpublishing.com
(719) 369-9050

Cover Design: David A. Martin, Middle Creek Publishing
Printed in the United States
Author Photo: Courtesy of

First Edition, 2017

ISBN: 978-0-9974200-9-8

Sawhorse
Tony Burfield
1. Human Ecology   2. Poetry   3. Colorado

Many of these poems have been previously published and are recorded in the Acknowledgments on page 27

Sawhorse

Tony Burfield

forward by David Anthony Martin

Middle Creek Publishing & Audio
Beulah, CO • USA

Forward

Sawhorse, the title of Tony Burfield's latest chapbook, comes from an expressive allusion in the poem of the same name; "Ripping apart an old pallet for sawhorse wood. The potentiality of sawhorse."

Sawhorse spans a year of newness, a marriage, a new house and a new sense of place as the poet embeds himself in the grounding process of work; the honest work of a homeowner, a landowner, a husband, a poet. This is the rurality of rediscovering the self in relationship to each other and to the land; the self as the *story* of place.

The poems comprising *Sawhorse* are rural, contemplative . . . simple, but not trite . . . and yet, Burfield is not *putting on any airs*, there are no claims to any mystic insight but for the simple newlywed sense of distracted joy, cramping muscles and newly calloused hands.

Burfield's dialect is distinct to the American mountain west. His prose poems are often clipped sentences, phrases and fragments, *just enough,* like the not-too-heavy, not-too-light layers worn by those of the mountain west to accommodate the swift changes of weather.

His palette is the lexicon of the foothills life zone, the mountains and canyons of Colorado's western slope; deer bones, cactus, ponderosa, grama grass (too real, *too rural* even for spellcheck), crags, canopy, pelvis, vertebrae, cord wood, fire rings, treeless peaks, switchbacks, snow, hermits, the dry heat, *the dry cold*, winters that mean business, stars, snowpack, aspen, sawdust and sap, slot canyon, flash-flood, wildfire and fear . . . parsing scat, feathers, blood and bone.

I found myself instinctively checking my socks for *hound's tongue* burrs when I finished reading it.

Sawhorse is an honest and concise chapbook. Twenty-four poems, mostly *haibun*, a pairing prose-poems and haiku. Reading Burfield's *haibun*, I was reminded of the Japanese word *fushi* (*bushi* 節) with it's etymological allusion to a knot or *whorl* in the grain of wood or bamboo, while also being the word for *song*; an eddy, ripple or the endless flow of the Universe, turning briefly back on itself.

Many works under the bumbershoot of 'ecopoetics' express the complexity of human impacts on our natural environments and ecologies. *Sawhorse* is a gesture that relates poetries to places, and of the poets work to comprehend and redefine our *placed-ness* in our natural ecology and *place-making* practices in our natural and built ecologies. This Button Rock House series chronicles an emerging *topophilia*, poetry as a form of inhabitance, and well-deserves a place in the environmental canon of the literary mountain west. Short, yes, and sweet at times, like life, like springtime in the rockies; full of possibility, full of potential.

David Anthony Martin
Founding Editor of Middle Creek Publishing & Audio
author of *Span, Deepening The Map,* and *Bijoux*.

Topophilia:

"The affective bond between people and place"— arising out of *"experiences mostly fleeting and undramatic, repeated day after day over a span of years."*

~Yi Fu Tuan,
  (1974:4)
  (1977: 183)

for Laura

Sawhorse

Unfletched

November

Our new home. We stack the old, wood-like deer bones in the back, among the hedgehog cactus, dry blue grama, and grey ponderosa cones. A pelvis, three femora, a vertebra. She picks the grasses for an inspiration cliff and I point the unfletched arrow, This Here! That There! This our first week at Button Rock House.

her smile —
I miss the doorknob
once, twice

Sawhorse

Burner

Rob Alm came today with a tri-axle of wood, asked us to firefighting and star-gazing, told us to just walk in, his wife at home welcoming all visitors, her farmer hands cool, her light hair afloat on wood stove heat. Rob Alm teaches juniper, doug fir.

old forehead bruise
under the woodshed
a low crouch

Tony Burfield

Criaturas

Late afternoon at Button Rock House. The snow comes down at angles. The crows, 40 or more, weave circular dives and glides all to flap and land in a single fir along our dirt road. The Slab, that treeless peak, is perfect in its snowbound tilt, and the canyon road flashes to white in one wind. A corvid call rings from the East. But Button Rock herself looms behind us with an opaque snow curtain hiding all the caves and toothy criaturas.

xmas eve —
crazy Frank hitching
down canyon

Sawhorse

one snow plop + one snow plop = one snow plop

Tony Burfield

Sawhorse

Ripping apart an old pallet for sawhorse wood. The potentiality of sawhorse. With screws and nails, hammer in hand, I crouch amid the wind and cold. Every so often, I look up from pulling nail heads off to admire the rocky crags and ponderosas and know grounded presence for the first time in my life, my true calling: Button Rock House.

winter evening —
piles of warm books
in the sunroom

Sawhorse

The Button Rock Hermit

The Button Rock hermit didn't know about Cold Mountain or Judevine until it was too late, but she did have a stick. On cold mountain nights, while walking the county dirt roads, she'd hold her stick up and shout, "Bah! Rah! Hah!" And from there, she'd shiver her way home.

fingerless gloves —
she stitches feathers
stitches teeth

Tony Burfield

With Human Feet

The wind last night, the fast thoughts all night of Jim the neighbor, a "basement wizard," his awkward talk and gossip about Carl, the water man. His boast about chasing a cougar through the boulders. "With human feet?," she asks afterward, and now today with the longer evening. The sun will warm the house until nearly 4pm.

what a joke,
all my bragging —
new snow on old

Sawhorse

winter night —
too cold to hold
the star chart

Tony Burfield

Dog First

This dry Colorado winter. Snow in spurts. It comes the day before the family arrives from the low country and so begins my shoveling. Snowpack melt-freezes into ice-rock, and I chip at it with shovel edge. Little chunks here and there. It takes hours and the callouses and the cramps and the clearing sky to blue and then from across the property bounds Shakes, whiskers iced and high in dog smiles, Dennis coming after. I greet the dog first and then the man.

grandad
teases about my soft hands —
the thick creek ice

Sawhorse

Goals

My teacher is my wife's press. Which of us will go first. It's a shitty no-win. So we sit and stretch. Stretching cuss words like Susan Howe up in grey Buffalo. My bitter diet of cranberries. The gaps as big as the page. Button Rock House. We're philistines. I walked the turkey-loop tonight without her. The gobblers, tail-feathers splayed, did their cock-tailed dance around the hens. Listen to the turtle snorgle. I'm not about to budge. It may be snowing, but my mind, right now, is sunny-side-up and I do want to be here.

leaf pieces —
worn list of goals
I had at 20

Tony Burfield

Blackberry Winter

Snowed-in. Two inches an hour. We called-in snowed-in. Weather radios for ease. The inches of white, feet of white. Verbless. Written in breath. We breathe. Verbed. Verbalizing our shivers in this crunchy month. Opened cans of tomatoes said all different in the forsaken East. We shovel and scrape. We dress our feet thick and the neighbor's dog in his blizzard booties.

the clouds
out there claws sink
into muscle

Sawhorse

spring snow —
she lets me share
her pocket

Tony Burfield

The Worth of Climb

Boulder Brook trail, we hike it almost by accident. The steep climb surprises with huge aspen, huge fir, and cascade after cascade, peppered with smooth grey water ouzels, and near the top, near the first camp, the canopy opens up to the high snowy peaks, jagged and cold even in the May sun. I gaze over the mountain snowscape and from behind my wife's whisper, she always closer to the earth, "There's a moose!"

a cloud
from dragon
back to cloud

Sawhorse

Can-O-Worms Trail

I hiked alone up Can-O-Worms Trail behind Meadow Peak. A cave up there behind a thicket, dry inside with cougar scat all around. I cut some up, all full of bone chunks and hair. Just at the mouth of the cave an old fire ring circles in stone, the char already back to dirt. Farther along, just down into Dry Gulch, just a few yards off trail, it stopped me still with awe and fear: a gnawed up and off elk leg, from the knee down, the hoof perfect and hard.

trail runner
with five dogs —
I clean my boot

Tony Burfield

On Cutting Wood for a Chair

Measure in threes, eye-ball twice, cut once. Measure in threes, the pencil lines across the reclaimed deck board. This square too small, that square too big. A look up into the cliffs, listen for the wind, an exhale. Eye-ball twice, step back, lean in. How long is my thumb? Set the board on my toe, the balance in bone. This wood is sound. And even a sniff at the pre-sawdust air. Cut once, the circ saw jumps into its wicked spin and chews right straight and blows into my face. Dusting off my hat, I appraise the cut and listen for the blade to stop: Splintered and rough.

a new worry
replaces an old one —
sunburn spring

Sawhorse

all the pollen caught
in the dandelion clock
wanderlust

Tony Burfield

Little Paws

Working the land today around the house, we clear brush, branches and trees from around the big boulder who we named "Little Paw," our saw blade hot and sappy. She works right through her gloves and all my blisters from last week's work tear away, painless. After we finish dragging everything down to the slash pile, we climb up top Little Paw and look out over the house and valley, up at the peaks. When there are mountains, we look at mountains. She sees a big lizard on a small boulder below, the first of the season.

juncos burst
from mountain folds —
a matter of style

Sawhorse

Tree-Sniffing, Scat-poker

Difference between bone and horn. Mother came and defied our dirt-worshipping. Her spine-snapped bible. The trail we hiked hid certain colors, but the Big Horn's curls... the stomp and rack twirl. From the morning West came light wind, wildfire smoke. Throat scratches and a scrawny Jesus. We hear you mum and still we sniff close to the trees.

now when the beta vixens
scream after midnight,

I simply
close
the window.

Tony Burfield

Crow Traffic

Mountain seeking. The early hike up deer loop. The buck all antler shed. We draw out a long post-tramp tea. Winds and snows patchwork across ice ground and brown shaking knapweed. This morning, this morning, mountain seeking and crow flight in tourist traffic.

my worries
in all her seasons
fire, flood

Sawhorse

Barn Cat Revival

I studied under her, under this or that bunkhouse muse. This song about dream redacted or speaking dream and poetry out to the wilderness, like how I used to speak with the kittens who slept outside the sunken windows in winter. Why count this kitten population, or the number of children I could have had. Count how the lips move, count the metaphors who are absent in the slot canyons. There, it's ice or nothing.

vasectomy —
50 white tiles
51 blue

Tony Burfield

my spirit animal
switchback
to fox

Sawhorse

Wild Two-Step

Slow hike up Dark Mountain. At the summit the ranges stretch one after another out of sight beyond the divide. Chasing my hermit again. The root caves sheltered in aspen, doug fir, but inside protected by cougar scat and deer bone. Gun shots from far off echo through forest and canyon. What is required for primal depth, how far can you chase a hermit before the slope gets too steep and your legs go noodle.

the thump
into the non-human
blood-feather dance

Tony Burfield

Trail Bones

The braided deer trails up Big Paw Peak lead under balanced rocks and rusted barbed wire and through endless deep duff. At the gully bottom a flood has driven stones and branches and bones. This is an old river and the ponderosa that loops still with a mess of feathers caught in the flaky bark, blood too and more bone. The bone of ages piled under foot, broken, healed and broken again by our boots treading and trod. These trail bones give a history more textured than any voice or book-word ever could.

elk antlers
in an intricate pile
talk of trust

Sawhorse

Possible House

November

One year marked at Button Rock House. Fires and flood blown through and now I fear that rain and sun and earth will close us. This is no warning or reprimand. Fact. As a boot to dirt or broken toe knuckle, fact as all of death and geologic second. "This is nothing" says old woman sky. "This is." We take all words and sit still, sip tea, and watch mountain clouds.

night mist
floats through unnoticed —
this possible house

Acknowledgements

Some of these poems, in slightly different forms, have appeared in, *Contemporary Haibun Online*, *The Heron's Nest*, *Lilliput Review* and *Modern Haiku*.

The poem, 'Little Paws,' is in homage to Santoka Taneda's work as translated by John Stevens.

I would like to express my gratitude to Innisfree Poetry Bookstore & Cafe in Boulder, Colorado on University Hill, one of three exclusively-poetry bookstores in the United States. Innisfree Poetry Bookstore & Cafe creates and fosters a daily, living space for lovers of poetry, of all ages.

Many of the poems in *Sawhorse* were revised and organized at Innisfree before my work shifts at the library, and mostly at their old location across the street from their present location.

About The Author

Tony Burfield lives with his wife in Pinewood Springs, Colorado, and works at the Boulder Public Library.

Middle Creek Publishing Titles

Span
by David Anthony Martin

Deepening the Map
by David Anthony Martin

Phases
by Erika Moss Gordon

Cirque & Sky
by Kathleen Willard

Messiah Complex and Other Stories
by Michael Olin-Hitt

Lessons from Fighting The Black Snake at Standing Rock
by Nick Jaina and Leslie Orihel

Wild Be
by One Leaf

Bijoux
by David Anthony Martin

Sawhorse
by Tony Burfield

Almost Everything, Almost Nothing
by KB Ballentine

ECO/CO Books is an imprint of Middle Creek Publishing & Audio publishing books about Colorado by Colorado authors.

Purchase of this book supports

Greenwood Wildlife Rehabilitation Center's mission is to rehabilitate orphaned, sick and injured wildlife for release into appropriate habitats. Greenwood also strives to educate the public, emphasizing humane solutions to human / wildlife interactions.

www.ingramcontent.com/pod-product-compliance
Lightning Source LLC
Chambersburg PA
CBHW022126090426
42743CB00008B/1021